M000305062

THIS NOTEBOOK BELONGS TO ....

CONTACT ....

Published and © copyright 2018 Flame Tree Publishing Ltd

FTNB72 • ISBN 978-1-78361-353-3

Cover image based on a detail from
American Gothic, 1930 by Grant Wood (1891–1942)
Courtesy Google Cultural Institute and © respective museum

Grant Wood's image of two stoic Iowa citizens in front of their home has become a classic of modern American art. At first glance it shows proud owners standing awkwardly in front of their pioneer homesteads. Wood, though, appears subtly to undermine the simplicity of the image with darker implications of the gothic window, the tricorn rake, and the severe expressions of the subjects.

FLAME TREE PUBLISHING | The Art of Fine Gifts
6 Melbray Mews, London SW6 3NS, United Kingdom